First World War
and Army of Occupation
War Diary
France, Belgium and Germany

28 DIVISION
Divisional Troops
3 Brigade Royal Field Artillery
16 November 1914 - 31 October 1915

WO95/2271/3

The Naval & Military Press Ltd
www.nmarchive.com
Published in association with The National Archives

Published by

The Naval & Military Press Ltd

Unit 10 Ridgewood Industrial Park,

Uckfield, East Sussex,

TN22 5QE England

Tel: +44 (0) 1825 749494

www.naval-military-press.com

www.nmarchive.com

This diary has been reprinted in facsimile from the original. Any imperfections are inevitably reproduced and the quality may fall short of modern type and cartographic standards.

© Crown Copyright
Images reproduced by permission of The National Archives, London, England, 2015.

Contents

Document type	Place/Title	Date From	Date To
Heading	WO95/2271-3		
Heading	3rd Brigade R.F.A. Dec 1914-Oct 1915		
Heading	3rd Bde. R.F.A. Vol I 16.11.14-30.1.15		
War Diary	Devonport	16/11/1914	16/11/1914
War Diary	Winchester	19/11/1914	12/01/1915
War Diary	Southampton	15/01/1915	15/01/1915
War Diary	Havre	16/01/1915	17/01/1915
War Diary	Pradelles	17/01/1915	28/01/1915
War Diary	Pradelles and Ypres	29/01/1915	29/01/1915
War Diary	Pradelles	30/01/1915	30/01/1915
Heading	3rd Bde. R.F.A. Vol II 1-28.2.15		
War Diary	Pradelles	01/02/1915	01/02/1915
War Diary	Ypres	02/02/1915	28/02/1915
Heading	3rd Brigade R.F.A. Vol III 1-31.3.15		
War Diary	Ypres	01/03/1915	31/03/1915
Heading	3rd Brigade R.F.A. Vol IV 1-30.4.15.		
Miscellaneous	Office Of Adjt General the Base	23/04/1915	23/04/1915
War Diary	Ypres	01/04/1915	10/04/1915
War Diary	Poperinghe	11/04/1915	11/04/1915
War Diary	Ypres	12/04/1915	30/04/1915
Heading	3rd Bde. R.F.A. Vol V 1.5.15-1.6.15		
War Diary	Ypres	01/05/1915	09/05/1915
War Diary	Vlamertinghe	09/05/1915	01/06/1915
Heading	3rd Bde R.F.A. Vol VI 1-20-6-15		
War Diary		01/06/1915	30/06/1915
Heading	3rd Brigade R.F.A. Vol VII 20-6-15-31-7-15		
War Diary		20/06/1915	31/07/1915
Heading	3rd Bde R.F.A. Vol VII From 1st to 31st Aug. 1915		
War Diary		01/08/1915	31/08/1915
Heading	3rd Bde R.F.A. Vol 9 Sept 15		
War Diary		01/09/1915	30/09/1915
Heading	War Diary 3rd Bde. R.F.A. 28th Div. From 1.10.15 To 31.10.15 Vol X		
War Diary		01/10/1915	31/10/1915

WO95/22711/3

28TH DIVISION
DIVL ARTILLERY

3RD BRIGDE R.F.A.
DEC 1914-OCT 1915

28th Division

3rd Bde. R.F.A.

Vol I. 16.11.14 — 30.1.15

121/4193

2 3 Rifle RRC

Army Form C. 2118.

WAR DIARY
or
INTELLIGENCE SUMMARY.
(Erase heading not required.)

Hour, Date, Place	Summary of Events and Information	Remarks and references to Appendices
16. Nov. 1914. DEVONPORT.	The Brigade arrived home from INDIA: introd. on the S.S. "NEURALIA"	
19. Nov. 1914. WINCHESTER.	Arrived at WINCHESTER by rail. Authors with camp at MAGDALEN HILL, where huts — for a single battery only of horses were received. Details to 28th Division. Moved into billets.	
17. Dec. 1914. WINCHESTER.		
20. Dec. 1914. WINCHESTER.	On reorganisation once/twice in following manner took place:— All Batteries transferring "6 guns" were limited into two batteries each of 4 guns — The Right half retaining the original Battery number. The left half becoming a new Battery — each receiving a fourth subsection gun. The Brigade thus became two Roman numbers being "3²" and "146²" — The Batt. so became:— 18. — 18ᵗ and 365. ⎫ The 18, 62 + 365 have 62. — 62 and 366. ⎬ formed the 3ʳᵈ Brigade. 75. — 75 and 367. ⎭ The 75, 366 + 367. The 146ᵗ Brigade —	

3rd Brigade RFA

WAR DIARY
or
INTELLIGENCE SUMMARY.

Army Form C. 2118.

Hour, Date, Place	Summary of Events and Information	Remarks and references to Appendices
22 Dec /14 – Jan 5 /14 Jan '15. WINCHESTER.	Mobilisation carried out. The 3rd Brigade RFA Ammunition column being formed.	
12 Jan '15 WINCHESTER.	The whole of the 28. Division relieved by 4th Division.	
15 Jan '15. SOUTHAMPTON.	The Brigade left WINCHESTER by route march for SOUTHAMPTON where it embarked:— HeadQuarters – in the "TRAFFORD HALL" 18 Battery – in the "NAVIAN" 62 Battery – in the "City of BENARES" 365 Battery – in the "Lake MICHIGAN" Ammunition Column in the "TINTORETTO"	
16, 17 Jan '15 HAVRE.	Disembarked – 18 & 65 Batteries on 16; remainder on 17 Jan – after a very rough passage –	
17th & 18 Jan 15 PRADELLES.	Railed to HAZEBROUCK, detraining there and marching into billets.	
2.30pm 23 Jan 15 PRADELLES.	Orders received – Brigade to be ready to move at two hours notice.	
28 Jan '15 PRADELLES.	The Brigade was inspected by F.M. Sir JOHN FRENCH Commander in chief.	

3rd Bde RFA

Army Form C. 2118.

WAR DIARY
or
INTELLIGENCE SUMMARY.

(3)

Hour, Date, Place	Summary of Events and Information	Remarks and references to Appendices
29. Jan. 1915 PRADELLES and YPRES	In view of the relief been need of the 3rd French Division by our 28th Division. Arrangements were made for Lieu. Polywart. Battery Commander and Reserve? Ammunition Officer to proceed YPRES and spend a day there with the Artillery which he are to replace.	
30 Jan. 1915 PRADELLES	Much valuable information was obtained and we moved PRADELLES on following day. (Attn)	

A.2

121/4468

28th Division.

3rd Bde: R.F.A.

Vol II. 1 — 28. 2. 15

3rd Bgde RFA

Army Form C. 2118.

WAR DIARY
or
INTELLIGENCE SUMMARY. (4)
(Erase heading not required.)

Instructions regarding War Diaries and Intelligence Summaries are contained in F.S. Regs., Part II and the Staff Manual respectively. Title pages will be prepared in manuscript.

Hour, Date, Place	Summary of Events and Information	Remarks and references to Appendices
7.20 am 1st Feb 15 PRADELLES	The Brigade (less the section instructing an ammunition column) marches at Pradelles to Hazebrouck S.E. & VLAMERTINGHE arriving about 7.0 pm. The guns were moved by night into position S.W. of YPRES in relief of similar number of guns French Artillery 56th Regt. Operation completed by 11.30 pm after considerable difficulty, owing to wet ground, etc. The remainder of the Brigade marched out and rejoined Headquarters as above. Wine Waggons. The Ammunition Column and horse (except 4 teams on duty as horse sharers) were billeted as above - Officers and sufficient personnel to man the guns - living with the guns - Others in a house. Men in shelter. Regis ration to allotted zone was ordered to be completed to day, but owing	
2 Feb 15 YPRES		O. Plumiring forms.

(73989) W4141—463. 400,000. 9/14. H.&J.Ltd. Forms/C. 2118/10.

WAR DIARY or INTELLIGENCE SUMMARY

Army Form C. 2118.

Sheet - (5)

Hour, Date, Place	Summary of Events and Information	Remarks and references to Appendices
3rd Feb 1915. YPRES.	to breaks in the wire from observation Station it was impossible to do so. The remaining FRENCH guns consequently were not withdrawn and there not being space for any more guns in pits and Capt C.W. Batterie. The sections of 18 prs and 62nd Batterie has to be parked for following day - particular consideration being taken to hide them from aerial observation. The guns of 365 were brought up into position. AE.W. More registration carried out but again great difficulty with telephone wire. A second line of humane wire was laid under the frost. Lt. J. E. WHITEHEAD. The FRENCH artillery completed their withdrawal. Remaining guns of 18 prs and 62 W Batteries brought up - completed by 10.0 pm. OE.W.	
4 Feb 1915. YPRES. 9.35 am	The FRENCH having been withdrawn. The Brigade was now prepared and ready to take part in operations. Telephone message from 83rd Infantry Brigade asking for assistance to get objective (being indicated off the square) made provided. This happened to be in the zone allotted to the 365th Battery and so to them nearly fell the honour of firing the Brigades first	

Army Form C. 2118.

Sheet (6.)

WAR DIARY
or
INTELLIGENCE SUMMARY.
(Erase heading not required.)

Hour, Date, Place	Summary of Events and Information	Remarks and references to Appendices
12.0 noon	round in the campaign. The Battery was quick in getting on, but opening of fire was delayed owing to the presence of hostile aircraft. There was very little firing required. About midday some GERMAN shell began to fall not far from us but apparently not intended for us. On this fire ceasing, the O.C. Brigade proceeded to Head Quarters 83rd Infantry Brigade remaining there throughout the day. There was not much firing during afternoon and action appeared to	
6.30 pm 8.0 pm	Cease about 6.30 pm. It was resumed however about 8.0 pm, our own three Batteries did a certain amount of firing, objectives indicated from the map. GW	
5 Feb. 1915	Batteries again standing to - throughout the day, but no shooting was required - the GERMAN aeroplanes very much more "in evidence" now that the only gun available for use against them is No 13 B.R.A. - 2 guns of the CHESTNUT Troop R.H.A. - not nearly so quick and as the FRENCH "75" Moreover, unable to get on a much elevation.	

WAR DIARY
or
INTELLIGENCE SUMMARY.
(Erase heading not required.)

Army Form C. 2118.

Sheet (7)

Hour, Date, Place	Summary of Events and Information	Remarks and references to Appendices
11.30 a.m.	Our Mr FRENCH Artillery Officer met on most emphatic in his opinion that in order to secure the safety of Our Battery, it is absolutely essential to keep hostile aircraft at a distance. The CO returned from 83rd Infantry Brigade having ordered Lieut. R.G. STICKLAND to go there in his place to represent him.	
2.40 p.m.	Secret orders received that CROC is to start attack of portion of the GERMAN Trench at 9.0 p.m tonight. Information also received that it is intended to assist CROC by taking 6 rifles & two guns to the Ridge —	
9.0 p.m GEO MONTE-	Fire opened on allotted zone — and kept up at intervals till 12.30 A.M. — the presence of an officer (Capt) at Our Bn. Infantry Head Quarters proves to be of greatest assistance — One good reason is :—	
	11.55 pm CROC — is in the Trenches — also forthcoming a certain shot.	
	12.0 m.n. The first round fired and both Batteries — 62" and 365" — joined in a rapid fire — which was later on ascertained to be accurate — "Great harm" being was done to the first line of the	
6 FEB 1915 Y PRES.		

Army Form C. 2118.

Sheet (8)

WAR DIARY
or
INTELLIGENCE SUMMARY.
(Erase heading not required.)

Hour, Date, Place	Summary of Events and Information	Remarks and references to Appendices
9.40 pm	GERMAN Trenches — the actual line being — a large extent obstructed. The fire effect was good. And there became hints we sent from the trenches to the Infantry Brigade (83rd) Headquarters. More than was received in one office and despatched from another.	O/S. O/S.
	Day passed uneventfully — Bus at 9.40 pm warned by 83rd Infantry Bde that help of one battery house batteries be required 10.0 pm by 15 Corps — a working party repairing a trench. 62´ Ration warned	
10. 0 pm	Ordered to open fire "occasional rounds" — and fire opened accordingly & kept up regularly till 10 p.m. when orders to cease fire were received.	O/S.
10.30 pm		
1. Feb 8.15. YPRES	Nothing to record. O/S.	
2. Feb 9.15. YPRES	Nothing to record. O/S.	
3. Feb 9.15. YPRES	An uneventful day — At 9.5 pm a message from 83rd Infty Brigade to our half — ~~[struck out]~~	O/S.
4. Feb 10.15. YPRES	Batteries were promptly ready — but fire was not required.	

WAR DIARY or INTELLIGENCE SUMMARY

Army Form C. 2118.

Sheet (9)

Hour, Date, Place	Summary of Events and Information	Remarks and references to Appendices
10. Feb. 1915 YPRES 8.30 am	Message from 85 Infantry Brigade advising for our fire - Shelled accordingly. Our continued artillery fire continued till 10.30 am	
10.30 am		
11.30 am	Visit from R. Crefus (?) Commander. Li. Col. an RA Staff Officer. The situation and resources for our Many observation of fire in cooperation with Infantry men discussed - followed by a visit to the Batteries	Chs
10.30 am 11 Feb 1915 YPRES 2.0 pm	Co visited T.O. of RA and Situation was discussed. Co interviewed Battery Commanders another - accompanied by Major STAKE - made an extra Site reconnaissance towards forward fartland on any suitable observation post - on the left - (2 West) No suitable position was found - On the left (near) Lt. BATES (RHA attached) reconnoitred to a post discussed post - Suitability a my given report -	Chs
10.30 am 12 Feb 1915 YPRES	This this intent office 2/L Strickland proceeded to the area to recommend (upgrade) Everything these out hosted out the places to be selected. The Co ordered these but O.C.s must be taken to prevent Wingaarde Croze.	Chs

WAR DIARY or INTELLIGENCE SUMMARY

Army Form C. 2118.

Sheet (a)

Hour, Date, Place	Summary of Events and Information	Remarks and references to Appendices
11.45 a.m. 12. Feb 1915 – YPRES	Ambassadors from G.O.C.R.A. the General on the Centre and left Column & the Zone allotted to the Brigade – at first an area in rear of the GERMAN trenches – later the trenches – On a require from 85 Infantry Brigade trenches from the Off. Railway – 85* – was given GERMAN trenches the Bry arose trenches whilst it established two batteries by the Mons. 6:10 pm Mo. 22. Bry RFA on application from 85 Infantry Brigade the was	
3.20 p.m		
11.30 p.m	thence to come to relief of men in trenches. G.O. requisitioned own detachiliipillar to Trust Battery – the prepared but not occupied for reasons Battery – to Nothing of any importance from trenches after	
13. Feb 1915 YPRES 7.0 a.m	A message received 7.0 am 85. Infantry Brigade asking for no fire during the night to enable parts repairing trenches. Complied with and we had fire keeps up.	
2.30 a.m. 14. Feb 1915 YPRES 8.0 a.m	Fire to Brigade ceases – have taken up 6 BELGIAN Artillery – Report from 85 Infantry Brigade that our fire has has desired effects –	

Army Form C. 2118.

Sheet (11)

WAR DIARY
or
INTELLIGENCE SUMMARY.
(Erase heading not required.)

Instructions regarding War Diaries and Intelligence Summaries are contained in F.S. Regs., Part II. and the Staff Manual respectively. Title pages will be prepared in manuscript.

Hour, Date, Place	Summary of Events and Information	Remarks and references to Appendices
11.0 a.m. 14 Feb 1915 YPRES 12.0 noon → 1.30 p.m.	Orders from G.O.C. R.A. to open fire on the right portion of Couple à Hut — the orders seem to be, Bns to be prepared to support infantry attack. Orders from G.O.C. R.A. to open fire in support of this attack — on the centre and right portions of Couple à Hut — General idea was our fire to continue with varying intensity till not—	
7.0 p.m.		
7.30 a.m. 15 Feb 1915 YPRES	Informed by C.R.A. that S. of attack previous day had failed & we opened to open fire on same at dawn. This fire maintained until 12.30 p.m., after which only occasional rounds fired. Carefully registered trench taken by Germans and a new to supporting down the relief by our Inf. Contempt. Opened rapid rate of fire and supports behind it trench handed it until 9.15	
8.00 p.m.		
16 Feb 1915 YPRES	Uneventful day. Relief of 85 Infantry Brig by 84th Infr Bde completed in night. No orderly hit. Means for 83rd Infantry Brigade say his attachment, during the night, without any infantry & RA, and that our fire would however probably be required etc. Note attached.	
8.15—		

Army Form C. 2118.

Sheet (2.)

WAR DIARY
or
INTELLIGENCE SUMMARY.
(Erase heading not required.)

Hour, Date, Place	Summary of Events and Information	Remarks and references to Appendices
9.0 p.m. 16 Feb 1915 YPRES.	Message from 85 Infy Bde called for reinforcements. Fire in use all. Firing ensued till 9.30 p.m.	
12.5. a.m. 17 Feb 1915 YPRES	Message from 85 Infy Bde to say about one in [illegible] intended; should be required - available at about 2.0 a.m. Three minutes 2.50 a.m. submission required and then 1st 25 minutes only.	
6.30 a.m.	Orders to open fire regularly & carefully with two howitzers. Fire opened & continued till 4.45 - as ordered.	
18 Feb 1915 YPRES	Nothing of interest.	
19 Feb 1915 YPRES.	Nothing of interest.	
20 Feb 1915 YPRES. 3.10 p.m.	22nd Battery arrived and went into billets. Kept in reserve.	
	Orders from Divisional Head Quarters to open fire on the scheme left [illegible] by me 3 a.m. - Complied with and fire kept up - at varying rate - till 6.30 p.m.	
12.40 a.m. 21 Feb 1915 YPRES.	Orders from Divisional Head Quarters to open fire at 1.2 & 4 a.m. extreme left of zone - Complied with; fire stopped at 1.20 a.m. under orders from Bde Headquarters	

Army Form C. 2118.

Sheet (13)

WAR DIARY
or
INTELLIGENCE SUMMARY.
(Erase heading not required.)

Instructions regarding War Diaries and Intelligence Summaries are contained in F.S. Regs., Part II. and the Staff Manual respectively. Title pages will be prepared in manuscript.

Hour, Date, Place	Summary of Events and Information	Remarks and references to Appendices
7.15 am 21st Feb 1915 YPRES	Fire on left of zone afar required – main fire west of Vorgenne intervals til 6.30 pm – (Sd)	
22 Feb. 1915 YPRES	Nothing of interest. (Sd)	
23 Feb 1915 YPRES	Nothing of interest. (Sd)	
24 Feb 1915 YPRES 9.15 am	Fire of one battery required on centre of zone. Keep down the enemy's head – a few rounds only –	
1.45 pm	Fire of two batteries called on centre (centre) required to alone halt advance on N.S. centre of zone. (Sd)	
25 Feb 1915 YPRES	Nothing of interest. (Sd)	
26 Feb 1915 YPRES	Nothing of interest. (Sd)	
27 Feb 1915 YPRES	~~[struck out]~~ was the order of the due infantry Brigade occupying the Rets Section of our line – the objects being to ensure cooperation. (Sd)	was placed directly
28 Feb 1915 YPRES	Nothing of interest. (Sd)	

28th Division

3rd Brigade R.F.A.

121/4779

Vol III. 1 – 31.3.15

Army Form C. 2118.

WAR DIARY
or
INTELLIGENCE SUMMARY.
(Erase heading not required.)

28 sheets (14)

Hour, Date, Place	Summary of Events and Information	Remarks and references to Appendices
1st May 1915 YPRES.	On redistribution of the 28th Divisional artillery, the 2nd Brigade RHA and the 37th (Howitzer) Battery RFA forms the Right Group under command of Lt. Col. ALWRIGHT - and allotted to the "Rifles" Infantry Brigade - RHQ Nothing further. QMS	
2nd May 1915 YPRES.	Nothing further. QMS	
3rd May 1915 YPRES.	Enemy cut or destroying wire entanglements at Freuzeel. A Section Y Bty carried out by 60 Battery RFA - 80 rounds expended - Enemy heavily inquired into more trenches - Arms dumping arms - Further reconnaissance made for a position cannot find an Bty to act as a good position - same 1500 yds close in rear - Switch to rebuilding. QMS	
4th May 1915 YPRES.	Nothing of further interest. QMS	
5th May 1915 YPRES.	Nothing of interest to record. QMS	
6th May 1915 YPRES.	Nothing to record. QMS	

Army Form C. 2118.

Sheet (15)

WAR DIARY
or
INTELLIGENCE SUMMARY.
(Erase heading not required.)

Instructions regarding War Diaries and Intelligence Summaries are contained in F.S. Regs., Part II. and the Staff Manual respectively. Title pages will be prepared in manuscript.

Hour, Date, Place	Summary of Events and Information	Remarks and references to Appendices
7 March 1915 YPRES	Nothing to report. *Ops*	
8 March 1915 YPRES	Nothing to report. *Ops*	
9 March 1915 YPRES.	One section (the "5cms") 22nd Battery R.F.A. moved by night into a position on north bank of canal, 1900 yds from enemy's trenches — the object being to cut wire entanglement at close range than the before. *Ops*	
4.0 am 10 March 1915 YPRES. 6.30 am	Sub gun 22" Battery R.F.A. in action in position nr VOORMEZEELE. 107th Ammunition Col. Section moved forward (again) opened fire — fired 9.10 am fing 95 rounds — Fuzes inquiries, his demand same was carried out.	
10.30 am	The gun 22. Battery R.F.A. opened fire. Fired 100 rounds. Effect reported good —	
6.0 pm	The Section on north of canal was withdrawn — one gun being sent to VOORMEZEELE. *Ops*	
11 March 1915 YPRES	Divisional operations — in which the (B) & 62 Batteries and one section 22 Battery took part. The former being employed to fire on enemy's supports — the latter on wire entanglement. This section was withdrawn after dark returning to billets. *Ops*	

Army Form C. 2118.

WAR DIARY
or
INTELLIGENCE SUMMARY.
(Erase heading not required.)

Instructions regarding War Diaries and Intelligence Summaries are contained in F.S. Regs., Part II and the Staff Manual respectively. Title pages will be prepared in manuscript.

28 sheet (16)

Hour, Date, Place	Summary of Events and Information	Remarks and references to Appendices
8.20 a.m. 12 March 1915 YPRES 9.15 a.m.	Operating with 15th Infantry Brigade — firing on the enemy's Trenches over which gone. Firing ceased — OKW	
2.20 p.m. 13 March 1915 YPRES	Operating with 75th Infantry Brigade — firing with enemy's Trenches over where gone — for about ten minutes.	
6.0 p.m.	Two guns 22 Battery brought up into position — about two hundred yards to left of main position — with a view to employment by night in case of the 15th being obliged to assist "working parties" etc — the object being to obviate risk of flashes giving away our main position. OKW	
5.40 p.m. 14 March 1915 YPRES	Orders from G.O.C. Infantry Brigade to fire on white of enemy's Trenches. A rapid rate of fire being maintained as it was believed the enemy was attacking — Rate gradually reduced and firing ceased — 6 p.m. OKW	
6.0 p.m. 5 March 1915 YPRES	Ordered to shell enemy's trenches in front of left Regt "27" Div. who were attacking. Rapid rate of fire for last minute & then to a slow rate for fifty minutes. Nothing else going on except during the day. OKW	

Army Form C. 2118.

WAR DIARY
or
INTELLIGENCE SUMMARY.
(Erase heading not required.)

Sheet (17.)

Instructions regarding War Diaries and Intelligence Summaries are contained in F.S. Regs., Part II. and the Staff Manual respectively. Title pages will be prepared in manuscript.

Hour, Date, Place	Summary of Events and Information	Remarks and references to Appendices
16 March 915 YPRES.	Nothing of interest.	
17 March 915 YPRES.	Nothing of interest.	
18 March 915 YPRES.	Nothing of interest.	
19 March 915 YPRES	Nothing of interest.	
20 March 915 YPRES	Nothing of interest.	
21 March 915 YPRES	Registration on unseen target with observation from Balloon.	
22 March 915 YPRES.	Nothing of interest.	
23 March 915 YPRES.	Nothing of interest.	
24 March 915 YPRES	Nothing of interest.	
25 March 915 YPRES	Nothing of interest.	
26 March 915 YPRES	Nothing of interest.	

Army Form C. 2118.

WAR DIARY
or
INTELLIGENCE SUMMARY.

(Erase heading not required.)

Instructions regarding War Diaries and Intelligence Summaries are contained in F.S. Regs., Part II. and the Staff Manual respectively. Title pages will be prepared in manuscript.

Sheet (8.)

Hour, Date, Place	Summary of Events and Information	Remarks and references to Appendices
27 March 1915 YPRES	Nothing of interest. C.S.W.	
28 March 1915 YPRES	Nothing of interest. C.S.W.	
29 March 1915 YPRES	Nothing of interest. C.S.W.	
30 March 1915 YPRES	Nothing of interest. C.S.W.	
31 March 1915 YPRES.	Nothing of interest. C.S.W.	

28th Division.

2nd Brigade R.F.A.

Vol IV 1 – 30.4.15.

Office of Adjt. General
The Base .... No. 10. d. 28/—

Reference my A.F. C.2118 3rd Brigade
RFA I have neglected that 7 lower ranks
to report casualties. These are:—
14 Feb — 1 Sergt. 1 Gr wounded.
15 "   1 Bombardier   "
17 "   1 Sergeant 2 Gunners wounded.
2 March 1 Bombardier wounded
3   "   2nd Lieut R.S. TICKELL 365th Battery wounded
7   "   1 Staff Sergeant Fitter, 1 Bombardier
        and 3 Gunners wounded.
9   "   1 Gunner wounded.
10 "   1 Bombardier wounded.
12 "   1 Driver wounded
13 "   1 Bombardier accidentally
        wounded.
20 "   1 Gunner wounded.

Kindly insert in original — I have un-
entered in my copy.
Division Trunk reported.

            A.W. Baker
            Lieut Colonel
            Cmdg 3 Bde RFA

Army Form C. 2118.

WAR DIARY
or
INTELLIGENCE SUMMARY.
(Erase heading not required.)

Instructions regarding War Diaries and Intelligence Summaries are contained in F.S. Regs., Part II. and the Staff Manual respectively. Title pages will be prepared in manuscript.

Sheet No/

Hour, Date, Place	Summary of Events and Information	Remarks and references to Appendices
1 April 1915 YPRES	Nothing of interest. OC	
2 April 1915 YPRES	Nothing of interest. OC	
3 April 1915 YPRES	Nothing of interest. OC	
4 April 1915 YPRES	Nothing of interest. OC	
5 April 1915 YPRES	Nothing of interest. OC	
6 April 1915 YPRES	Nothing of interest. OC	
7 April 1915 YPRES	Nothing of interest. 10 W 25 OC	
8 April 1915 YPRES	Nothing of particular interest. Relief of 2nd Divisional Artillery commenced. A section from each of 119, 120 & 122 Batteries coming up in relief of 3rd Bty 2nd RCA. Their guns were to remain in position and ours withdrawn — OC	
1.0 am 9 April 1915 YPRES	Reconnaissance of the section withdrawn. Was night & all spare men horses & teams of Batteries marches to	
12 noon 10 April 1915	Capinny to Rest — It was of POPERINGHE. The Ammunition Column marches to new billets just east of VLAMERTINGHE	
9.0 am	Remaining section withdrawn about 11.0 am and rejoined	
11.0 pm	at its new billets west of POPERINGHE. OC	

Army Form C. 2118.

WAR DIARY
or
INTELLIGENCE SUMMARY.
(Erase heading not required.)

Instructions regarding War Diaries and Intelligence Summaries are contained in F.S. Regs., Part II. and the Staff Manual respectively. Title pages will be prepared in manuscript.

Sheet (20)

Hour, Date, Place	Summary of Events and Information	Remarks and references to Appendices
9.30 a.m 11 April 1915 POPERINGHE 6.30 p.m	Visit from Col. Von Walter.	
12 April 1915 12 April 1915 YPRES	1st, 92 & 62 Batteries (less one section) moved off to take over positions held by French Artillery about three miles east of YPRES. One Gunner wounded. Attn. Headquarters and remaining sections so above. Commr. held relief of French Artillery. Registration carried out. Both running was to the sections in turn. O&S one ammn. waggon was hit by enemy shrapnel..	
14 April 1915 15 April 1915 YPRES	Nothing of interest. O&S	
6.10 - 9.10 17 April 1915 YPRES 7.30	Nothing of interest. O&S	
	A demonstration by 28th Division in which the 72nd Battery took part. Fire from 7.30 & 7.40 p.m. on the front line and support trenches of the enemy at and just west of NOORDEMDHOOK. O&S	
18 April YPRES	Nothing of interest. O&S	
19 April YPRES	Nothing of interest. A.S.O. One gunner was missing. O&S	
20 April YPRES	Nothing of interest. A.S.O. Lieut. C.E.F. Revr. "K" Bty. Canadian Field Artillery arrived in camp and was placed on duty	

Army Form C. 2118.

(Sheet 2)

WAR DIARY
or
INTELLIGENCE SUMMARY.
(Erase heading not required.)

Instructions regarding War Diaries and Intelligence Summaries are contained in F.S. Regs., Part II. and the Staff Manual respectively. Title pages will be prepared in manuscript.

Hour, Date, Place	Summary of Events and Information	Remarks and references to Appendices
21. April 1915. YPRES.	In accordance with Secret orders received last night i.e. Gun ammee carried out for a position to be occupied by 365. Battery. Un resting - from which the Centre Group to bear on the country - about a mile East to South of ZONNEBEKE. Qty. Gun emplacements. Qty.	
22 April 1915 YPRES.	A quiet day as far as 3rd Brigade RCA concerned. but heavy firing - gun and rifle - on left. Enemy apparently trying to break through portion of line held by CANADIAN Division and ALGERIAN Troops. This confirmed by news later in evening	
3.30 p- 23 April 1915	In neighbourhood our movements order from 83rd Infantry Brigade. French advance batteries opened on wide section. Under orders as above fire on night and centre portion	
3.27 p-	to rectir ceased -	
3.50 p-	All reported quiet and fire on left portion ceased - Qty	
8.30 A.M. 24 April 1915 YPRES.	A request from O.C. 146th Brigade for ammunition for CANADIAN artillery. Three wagons two machine 62- Battery opened to go and the ammunition was brought through ZILLEBEKE - the teams + wagons getting back safely to billets. Owing to absence of our own aeroplanes and the want of Anti Air Craft guns the enemy planes were able to	

WAR DIARY
INTELLIGENCE SUMMARY

Army Form C. 2118.

9 Lees 22

Hour, Date, Place	Summary of Events and Information	Remarks and references to Appendices
2.5 April 1915 YPRES 2.30 a.m.	Made a through reconnaissance - located portion of 62 Battery which was a accurate Shelled - No casualties in the Battery but in drawing late supply in (Crew) the supply & ammunition No 12305 Bdr Loopmans & J. FRAMPTON registed — Two Drivers & One waggon Gunner slightly wounded on 9.3". Q.T.W. Confidential orders for increase in levels of a withdrawal - CO & Major LEWIN reconnoitred road. Q.T.W.	
26 April 1915 YPRES 9.0 a.m.	CO accompanied by an Officer from each battery selected positions to N.W. of YPRES - During the morning a request from CRA 27 Div. for as many guns as possible could be spared to be showing rounds short North Croc R.B. Lefty Brigade decided that only four guns could be spared - two (18s and 4.5s) — showing rounds - latter was to a fresh position (J.23)	
3.45 pm	At request of OC 3rd Brigade RFA — with Rt Lefty Brigade fire of these four guns opened on enemy's wire of GRAVENSTAFEL firing for an hour. again later for about ten minutes Cha. Q.Sy.	

Army Form C. 2118.

Sheet (23)

WAR DIARY
or
INTELLIGENCE SUMMARY.
(Erase heading not required.)

Instructions regarding War Diaries and Intelligence Summaries are contained in F.S. Regs., Part II. and the Staff Manual respectively. Title pages will be prepared in manuscript.

Hour, Date, Place	Summary of Events and Information	Remarks and references to Appendices
27 April 1915. YPRES	Nothing to report — OH.	
28 April 1915. YPRES	Capt. T.F. SANDEMAN reported his arrival — believed as extra Capt. (No orders received) the man immediately detailed by R.A. to perform duties ADJUTANT — adjutant and Regt. RS.O. — OH.	
29 April 1915. YPRES about 4.0 am	The billet of the 62= Battery "Bayonline" & Capt S Kellie, and Casualties were one Driver killed = one officer 2nd Lieut S. ETHELSTON — one gunner and three drivers wounded — Capts horses and one mule killed or destroyed on account of wounds. Wagonline moved to 6 ans Mon Jours. OH	
30 April 1915. YPRES	Reconnaissance for Battery east of YPRES carried out. Wagonline billet of 2.D. Battery burned this evening — result hostile fire. One driver unconscious and two drivers severely wounded and several horses burned to death and destroyed. OH.	

(73989) W.4141—463. 400,000. 9/14. H.&J.Ltd. Forms/C. 2118/10.

121/5775.

28th Division.

3rd Bde: R.F.A.

Vol V 1 June 5 —— 1.6.15.

Army Form C. 2118.

WAR DIARY
or
INTELLIGENCE SUMMARY.
(Erase heading not required.)

Instructions regarding War Diaries and Intelligence Summaries are contained in F. S. Regs., Part II. and the Staff Manual respectively. Title pages will be prepared in manuscript.

Hour, Date, Place	Summary of Events and Information	Remarks and references to Appendices
1 May 1915 YPRES	Under instructions from 28th Divl. Artillery D2 Divl C.R.R & R.A. and F.C.I. WOODGATE sent to 146: Bony ade R.F.A. to make good casualties in action and (2) No conversance for that position as the wires back, faced N.N.W. East consistent. Ctri.	
2 May 1915 YPRES 6.30 am 6.0 pm	So on orders to prepare for move tonight. % Meredith & each battery to position in hour - rather at present from there used catti relation. Some Daachi. artillery fire and 5 Sergeant - one actg Bombardier and 5 Gunners - 22. RFA wounded.	
5.10 pm	Orders for withdrawal of Meredith battery Received - One section most M. decuring - O.S.J. receives - One section most M. decuring -	
3 May 1915 7.30 am	Instruments a request fm O.C. left & road 135 front line with juice 18' + 22' Batteries asked in support & left & P.S. Night Post - and continued throughout all about 70 pm Ctri	
3.55 -	Orders to conduct bright move & reinforce... and battere ... got out goth with orders & positions & received noise in YPRES as the Germans were gassing the ground around Ctri	
4 May 1915 YPRES	Batteria in action to all day. Casualties 1 Gunner killed Coopr 2 Gunners wounded - Ctri	
5 May 1915 YPRES	Col H.Q. moved out Km H.Q. & E.3 'Infront the hub into N.E. of YPRES Batterie in action for the whole day. - Assisting in repelling enemy attack in centre by 30 in allotted. One Sergeant wounded. P.T.O.	
6 May 1915 YPRES	Establishment of Batterie increased 3850 (SD2) dated 28 April 1915 - All Mines	

(73989) W4141-463. 400,000. 9/14. H.&J.Ltd. Forms/C. 2118/10.

Army Form C. 2118.

WAR DIARY
or
INTELLIGENCE SUMMARY.
(Erase heading not required.)

Instructions regarding War Diaries and Intelligence Summaries are contained in F.S. Regs., Part II. and the Staff Manual respectively. Title pages will be prepared in manuscript.

Hour, Date, Place	Summary of Events and Information	Remarks and references to Appendices
5 May 1915 Ypres	Then 8 in & 2" battery had remained silent all day & about M.G. Sniping forward inspected to keep them in action after 6.30 pm. but had to cease to be in readiness to deal with it at (all ?) remained quiet tonight.	
6 May 1915 Ypres	In action again throughout the day. Our W.B.L. 3rd Cavalry HR.	
7 May 1915 Ypres	Establishment of officers & batteries to be followed in the future on an established of 75 batteries, rather a large number retaining the ambulance (routine orders). There was no action on our side (& h. inf. — att.)	
8 May 1915 Ypres	Again wounded off & Roar ambulance car from the unit, further the h. Rings along W.H.O. just as enemy started to open fire. The shells burst fatally on captain G.W. & B. and just from the guns in & in action. Ratcliffe had all nearly killed. Some from just our Kilshaw's driver W.H.T. There were only 5 buffer muffles only three of the Rodney 193 only one car for use. Battery had four of its 22 Rodens and from & 62 Rodens. Waggon left in action. Officers & men others were wanted for the 75 Pauhs. waited & look to ? replace 62 (which had its leg blown considerably on flame). Reconnaissance on for the Poelcap. front.	

Army Form C. 2118.

WAR DIARY
or
INTELLIGENCE SUMMARY.
(Erase heading not required.)

Instructions regarding War Diaries and Intelligence Summaries are contained in F.S. Regs., Part II. and the Staff Manual respectively. Title pages will be prepared in manuscript.

Hour, Date, Place	Summary of Events and Information	Remarks and references to Appendices
	CASUALTIES WERE :-	
	18ᵗʰ Battery. 2/Lt. J. L. MAXWELL. 2/Lt. J. H. McDONALD. 1 Sergt.	
	1 Corporal 1 Bombardier 1 acting Bombardier and 6 gunners wounded.	
	25ᵗʰ Battery 2 gunners wounded and 1 gunner 365ᵗʰ Battery	
	attached - also wounded -	
	62ⁿᵈ Battery : 2/Lt. E. EDGINGTON and 2/Lt. J. L. CAMPLIN -	
	1 Sergt. 2 Bombardiers 1 acting Bombardier 6 gunners killed.	
	1 Sergt. 1 Corporal 2 acting Bombardier 9 gunners 2 drivers	
	wounded -	
9ᵗʰ May. 1915	Orders 1.20 a.m. orders to withdraw the whole Brigade to	
YPRES	west of YPRES to withdraw in order of 10 Corps Reserve.	
1.30 a.	Teams arrived about 3.0 a.m. and all batteries were	
	withdrawn without further [?]. Immediately afterwards	
VLAMERTINGHE	taken to overhaul equipment and ascertain amount	
	of the 16 guns only 4 serviceable 8 requiring extensive	
	repairs and 4 irreparable & batteries.	
10 May 1915	Resting and overhauling equipment.	
VLAMERTINGHE		
11 May 1915	Resting and overhauling equipment.	
VLAMERTINGHE		
12 May 1915	Resting and overhauling equipment. 18ᵗʰ Battery handed over	
Thurs. R 22 May	to "Duffus Group". On 21ˢᵗ May Lt.Col.T. Honeyford to
	command of Brigade. Lt.Col. Walker invalided[?].	

WAR DIARY
or
INTELLIGENCE SUMMARY.

(Erase heading not required.)

Army Form C. 2118.

Instructions regarding War Diaries and Intelligence Summaries are contained in F.S. Regs., Part II. and the Staff Manual respectively. Title pages will be prepared in manuscript.

Hour, Date, Place	Summary of Events and Information	Remarks and references to Appendices
6 a.m. 24th May 1915	Bde. moved into action WEST of YPRES in rear and 2nd new registered by Batteries. M 52nd Battery two howitzers hit by German 5"9 howitzer and in shell holed in Gun Line destroying a little equipment and wounding no men. M	
25th	The 18th Battery two howitzers shelled by 11" Howitzers Casualties very light 2 men slightly wounded. W	
26th	Nothing to report. Reconnaissances made of G.H.Q. line from MENIN ROAD - POTYZE. W	
27th - 31st June	Bde. started from west taking refuge by 34th Bde.	
August 1st June	Relief completed August Bushing & Battalion Area - West of WOTAB	
Night 3rd June		

28th Division

121/6356

3rd Bde R.F.A.
Vol VI
1-20-9-15

Army Form C. 2118.

WAR DIARY
or
INTELLIGENCE SUMMARY.
(Erase heading not required.)

Instructions regarding War Diaries and Intelligence Summaries are contained in F.S. Regs., Part II. and the Staff Manual respectively. Title pages will be prepared in manuscript.

Hour, Date, Place	Summary of Events and Information	Remarks and references to Appendices
1st June. 1915.	Nothing to report. Reconnaissance made of line from MENIN ROAD - POTYZE	R.O.C.
Night of 2nd/3rd June.	One section from each battery relieved by 34th Bde.	R.O.C.
Night of 3rd/4th June.	Relief completed & Brigade marched to Billeting Area West of WATOU.	R.O.C.
4th to 16th June.	Resting, completing establishment of horses & personnel over hauling guns. Two guns had to go to 10M for repair.	R.O.C.
16th June.	O C Brigade proceeded to KEMMEL & LA CLYTE with C.R.A. to reconnoitre position held by the 46th Bde R.O.C.	R.O.C.
17th June.	Battery Commanders ― do ―	R.O.C.
18th & 19th June.	One Section relieved a corresponding section of the 46th Bde.	R.O.C.
19th & 20th June.	Relief completed	R.O.C.
20th June	Registration completed on the day. Nothing of interest	R.O.C.

10/4/96

28th Division

3rd Punjab R.F.A.

Lt XII

2.0-6-31-7-15

a2
a86

3rd Brigade R.F.A.
28th Division

Army Form C. 2118.

WAR DIARY
or
INTELLIGENCE SUMMARY.
(Erase heading not required.)

Hour, Date, Place	Summary of Events and Information	Remarks and references to Appendices
20th June – 30th June	Nothing of interest	
1st July	A dummy battery was placed in position by 22nd Battery and one gun of the 18th Battery was placed in a forward position to enfilade German trenches near BOIS QUARANTE and HOLLANDSCHE-SCHUUR F.M.	
1st July – 7th July	Nothing of interest	
8th July	Captain R.F. ADAM joined from 4/1st Battery, 3rd Division and took over Adjutant of Brigade.	
9th July – 14th July	Nothing of interest	
15th July 6.30 a.m.	German aeroplane dropped smoke balls, and ranged a battery on dummy battery.	
8.35 p.m.	62nd & 365th Battery fired on German trenches in reply to calls from Infantry consequent on a German mine being exploded. The mine did no damage to our trenches.	

Army Form C. 2118.

WAR DIARY
or
INTELLIGENCE SUMMARY.
(Erase heading not required.)

Instructions regarding War Diaries and Intelligence Summaries are contained in F.S. Regs., Part II. and the Staff Manual respectively. Title pages will be prepared in manuscript.

Hour, Date, Place	Summary of Events and Information	Remarks and references to Appendices
15th, 18th July	Nothing of interest.	RR.
19th July	18th Battery fired with an observer in aeroplane to test new system of ranging	RR.
	22nd Battery ranged from kite balloon	
20th July	62nd Battery ranged from kite balloon.	RR.
21st July	18th Battery fired with aeroplane, as a further test of new system.	RR.
22nd July	62nd & 22nd Battery fired with aeroplane	RR.
	365 fired with balloon.	RR.
23 – 25 July	Nothing of interest	RR.
26th July	62nd Battery moved South & were attached temporarily to 146th Brigade till the Brigade moves down.	RR.
27th July	B/79 Battery, 17th Division took over 62nd Battery's position & came temporarily under of O.C. 3rd Brigade.	RR.

Army Form C. 2118.

WAR DIARY
or
INTELLIGENCE SUMMARY.

(*Erase heading not required.*)

Instructions regarding War Diaries and Intelligence Summaries are contained in F.S. Regs., Part II. and the Staff Manual respectively. Title pages will be prepared in manuscript.

Hour, Date, Place	Summary of Events and Information	Remarks and references to Appendices
28 – 31st July	Nothing of interest	

121/6550

28th Division

8nd Bde R.F.A.
Vol XIII
From 1st to 31st Aug. 1915

Army Form C. 2118.

WAR DIARY
or
INTELLIGENCE SUMMARY.
(Erase heading not required.)

Instructions regarding War Diaries and Intelligence Summaries are contained in F.S. Regs., Part II. and the Staff Manual respectively. Title pages will be prepared in manuscript.

Hour, Date, Place	Summary of Events and Information	Remarks and references to Appendices
1st - 6th August	Nothing of Interest	RPC
Night 6/7th	One Section 62nd Battery relieved one Section B/79th Battery, as movement of Brigade southwards had been cancelled	RPC
Night 7th/8th	Relief of B/79th by 62nd Battery completed. B/79th Battery marched to rejoin its own Brigade.	RPC
8th August	A/73 Howitzer battery joined the Brigade, and moved into billets till their inspection to prepared	RPC
9th August 3.0 a.m.	Bombardment of SPANBROEK MOLEN to assist attack made by 6th Divn in HOOGE. 18th Battery enfilade gun took part, other batteries did not fire	RPC

Army Form C. 2118.

WAR DIARY
or
INTELLIGENCE SUMMARY.
(Erase heading not required.)

Instructions regarding War Diaries and Intelligence Summaries are contained in F. S. Regs., Part II. and the Staff Manual respectively. Title pages will be prepared in manuscript.

Hour, Date, Place	Summary of Events and Information	Remarks and references to Appendices
10th – 13th August	Nothing of Interest	R.O.L
14th August	A/73 Battery having completed position reports at. commenced regis taken	R.O.L
15th – 19th August	Nothing of Interest.	R.O.L
20th August	Major E O Lewin commanding 18th Battery R.F.A. left the brigade on appointment to Brigade Major R.A. 12th Division.	R.O.L
21st – 24th August	Nothing of Interest	R.O.L
25th August	Major J. S. Cape posted to brigade to command 18th Battery R.F.A. from 31st Brigade Amm Column. Captain J. H. Macgregor from 18th Battery posted to command 31st Brigade Am: Column	R.O.L
26th August	Nothing of interest to report.	R.O.L

Army Form C. 2118.

WAR DIARY
or
INTELLIGENCE SUMMARY.
(Erase heading not required.)

Instructions regarding War Diaries and Intelligence Summaries are contained in F.S. Regs., Part II. and the Staff Manual respectively. Title pages will be prepared in manuscript.

Hour, Date, Place	Summary of Events and Information	Remarks and references to Appendices
27th August.	2/Lieut A. H. G. Giles joined the brigade from the base and was posted to 18th Battery.	RPh
28th – 31st August	Nothing of Interest to report.	RPh.

12/7051

38th Karoun

3rd Bde R.F.A.

Vol XIII 9
Sept. 15

Army Form C. 2118.

WAR DIARY
or
INTELLIGENCE SUMMARY.
(Erase heading not required.)

Instructions regarding War Diaries and Intelligence Summaries are contained in F.S. Regs., Part II. and the Staff Manual respectively. Title pages will be prepared in manuscript.

Hour, Date, Place	Summary of Events and Information	Remarks and references to Appendices
1st September	Nothing of interest to report.	R.O.a.
12th September		R.O.a.
13th September	365th Battery and 62nd Battery ranged by Captain P.G. Yorke. 365 Battery from the Balloon on points behind WYTSCHAETE ridge.	R.O.a.
14th September	Nothing of interest to report.	R.O.a.
15th September	Captain Yorke ranged 18th Battery and C.130th Howitzer Battery from Balloon.	R.O.a.
16th - 17th Sept	Nothing of interest to report.	R.O.a.
18th September	Orders as to relief of 28th Division by 2nd Canadian Division.	R.O.a.
19th September	Nothing of interest to report.	R.O.a.

Army Form C. 2118.

WAR DIARY
or
INTELLIGENCE SUMMARY.
(Erase heading not required.)

Instructions regarding War Diaries and Intelligence Summaries are contained in F.S. Regs., Part II. and the Staff Manual respectively. Title pages will be prepared in manuscript.

Hour, Date, Place	Summary of Events and Information	Remarks and references to Appendices
20th September	A section on 18th & 22nd Batteries relieved by D & B at 8 p.m.	ROC
21st September	Batteries respectively of 80th Brigade 17th Divn win. Relieved section return to their wagon lines. Staff Captain, 83rd Infantry Brigade allotted billets to 32nd Brigade R.F.A. in the neighbourhood of OUTERSTEEN. Section of 80th Brigade regs to trod front. One Section of 118th Brigade affords Canadian 1st Dunion relieved C 130th Battery.	ROC
22nd September		ROC
22nd September	Reaming sections of 80th Brigade relieved 18th & 22nd Batteries at 8 p.m. 62nd & 365th Batteries withdrew at 9 p.m. to their wagon lines, these batteries were not relieved. C/130th Battery withdrew & came under orders of O.C. 130th Brigade. At 9 p.m. Command handed over to O.C. 80th Brigade. ROC	

Army Form C. 2118.

WAR DIARY
or
INTELLIGENCE SUMMARY.
(Erase heading not required.)

Instructions regarding War Diaries and Intelligence Summaries are contained in F. S. Regs, Part II. and the Staff Manual respectively. Title pages will be prepared in manuscript.

Hour, Date, Place	Summary of Events and Information	Remarks and references to Appendices
23rd September	23rd Brigade R.F.A. marched at 10.30 a.m. to new billeting area via LOCRE, CROIX de POPERINGHE, METEREN. being inspected on the march by G.O.C. R.A. 28th D[ivision] www. Arrived at new billets at 3 p.m. Orders received for all units to be prepared to move at one hour notice. C.R.A. held conference of Brigade Commanders at 8.30 p.m.	R.C.
24th September	Orders received that one battery to be prepared to move at one hour notice, other units at short notice.	R.C.

Army Form C. 2118.

WAR DIARY
or
INTELLIGENCE SUMMARY.
(Erase heading not required.)

Instructions regarding War Diaries and Intelligence Summaries are contained in F.S. Regs., Part II. and the Staff Manual respectively. Title pages will be prepared in manuscript.

Hour, Date, Place	Summary of Events and Information	Remarks and references to Appendices
25th Sept.	Brigade remained in billets, orders to be ready to move at 2 hours notice.	RQ
26th Sept.	Orders received at 4 a.m. to move off at 6.0 a.m. with 83rd Infantry Brigade. Head of 3rd Brigade RQ. passed starting point OUTERSTEEN Cross Roads at 6.30 a.m. Marched to billets NW of MERVILLE. On arrival orders received to continue march to billets near ROBECQ. Brigade billeted 1½ miles NW of ROBECQ at 12 noon. Orders received at 1.0 p.m. to continue march on LOCON-HINGES area, after marching for an hour, orders cancelled & brigade returned to billets in ROBECQ.	RQ
27th Sept.	83rd Infantry brigade entrained at 1 p.m. for BETHUNE 3rd Brigade RQ marched at 2 p.m. to billets W	Off

WAR DIARY
or
INTELLIGENCE SUMMARY.
(*Erase heading not required.*)

Army Form C. 2118.

Instructions regarding War Diaries and Intelligence Summaries are contained in F.S. Regs., Part II. and the Staff Manual respectively. Title pages will be prepared in manuscript.

Hour, Date, Place	Summary of Events and Information	Remarks and references to Appendices
28th Sept	of HINGES for night.	RM
	Orders to move one battery to VERMELLES in combn. battery to be attached to 2nd Heavy Brigade, R.G.A. 18th Battery left billets at 7.30am in wildon one 18pr section of 3rd Bde A.C. and occupied position near VERMELLES coming under orders of O.C. 2nd Heavy Brigade R.G.A.	RM
29 Sept	Orders received for B.C.s and one officer per battery to report to H.Q. 52nd Brigade R.F.A. in order to be prepared to take over their positions. Capt [struck] Adjutant, & Battery officers reported at 8.0am & were taken round ———— by gun positions. C.O. & adjutant went to Cabret hfy Bde H.Q. where to leave situation. Bombardment fiery on in HOHENZOLLERN REDOUBT Party returned to billets at night	RG
30th Sept	B.C.s and one officer per battery as were attached to 52nd Brigade Batteries. One section from 22,62nd, 365th Batteries sectional came into action in relief of C, B & A Batteries 52nd Brigade but guns were exchanged between batteries	RG
		[signature] Colonel Cmdg RA
		Col 3rd Bde RGA

Volume No. 1

121
Medit
661

MEDITERRANEAN EXPEDITIONARY FORCE.

WAR DIARY.

28th Div

Unit 3rd Bde R.F.A. 28th Div

From 1.10.15   To 31.10.15

Vol. I

Actions during
October against
Hohenzollern &
Big & Little Willies

3rd Brigade RFA.

WAR DIARY
or
INTELLIGENCE SUMMARY.
(Erase heading not required.)

Army Form C. 2118.

Instructions regarding War Diaries and Intelligence Summaries are contained in F.S. Regs., Part II. and the Staff Manual respectively. Title pages will be prepared in manuscript.

Hour, Date, Place	Summary of Events and Information	Remarks and references to Appendices
1st October 12 noon	Remaining Sections of 22nd, 62nd, 365th batteries came into action attack in relief of remaining section 53rd Brigade. Brigade H.Q. moved up to H.Q of 52nd Brigade and Command was assumed for 12 hours.	
	C/130th Battery came under orders of the O.C. 3rd Bde. Batteries in action all day firing a barrage on GERMAN TRENCHES.	R.K.
8 pm	Fire opened on DUMP TRENCH in support of attack on LITTLE WILLIE TRENCH at battery fire 30 seconds 84th Brigade attacked successfully.	
2nd October 4.15 am	All batteries fired 5 rds gunfire on DUMP TRENCH to stop counter attack	
4.20 am	Fire stopped	
7 am	Fire commenced on communication trenches & kept up intermittently throughout the day. During the day Enemy again bombed their way into	R.K.

Army Form C. 2118.

WAR DIARY
or
INTELLIGENCE SUMMARY.
(Erase heading not required.)

Instructions regarding War Diaries and Intelligence Summaries are contained in F. S. Regs., Part II. and the Staff Manual respectively. Title pages will be prepared in manuscript.

Hour, Date, Place	Summary of Events and Information	Remarks and references to Appendices
	LITTLE WILLIE.	
8.0 p.m.	Battery fire one minute opened on DUMPTRENCH, FOSSE COTTAGES & NORTH FACE to prepare for an assault by 84th Infantry Brigade on LITTLE WILLIE	
8.10 p.m.	Rate increased to battery fire 20 seconds.	
8.30 p.m.	Fire stopped	
	As attack did not come off, the above operation was repeated at 9.45, 10.10 & 10.30 p.m.	
10.30 p.m.	Fire stopped at 10.30 p.m.	
3rd October		
12.30 a.m.	84th Brigade attacked without artillery support but were stopped by searchlight & enfilade machine gun fire.	RGC
5 a.m.	22nd & 62nd on LITTLE WILLIE Battery fire 30 seconds to prepare for a second attack by 84th Brigade	RGC

(73989) W4141—463. 400,000. 9/14. H.&J.Ltd. Forms/C. 2118/10.

WAR DIARY
or
INTELLIGENCE SUMMARY.
(Erase heading not required.)

Army Form C. 2118.

Instructions regarding War Diaries and Intelligence Summaries are contained in F. S. Regs., Part II. and the Staff Manual respectively. Title pages will be prepared in manuscript.

Hour, Date, Place	Summary of Events and Information	Remarks and references to Appendices
5.30am	Fire stopped as it got too light for attack to take place.	
7.30am	Enemy attacked our front line trench from LITTLE WILLIE. 22nd Battery & 62 Battery opened rapid fire on LITTLE WILLIE. 18, 366 & C/130 on communication trenches.	
7.50am	Report received that Enemy had been driven back.	
8.50am	Fire kept up on support & communication trenches during the day. 84th RFA Brigade relieved by 83rd Bde HFs Brigade during the day. WEST FACE lost to the enemy. Fire continued all night at rate of 4 rounds an hour to prepare for Assault by 83rd Infantry Brigade on WEST FACE.	
9 p.m.		
4th October		
4.30am	Assault by 83rd Infantry Brigade on WEST FACE unsuccessful.	
5.30am	All batteries firing on enemy trenches communication trenches Battery fire 30 seconds.	RBC

WAR DIARY
or
INTELLIGENCE SUMMARY.
(Erase heading not required.)

Army Form C. 2118.

Instructions regarding War Diaries and Intelligence Summaries are contained in F.S. Regs., Part II. and the Staff Manual respectively. Title pages will be prepared in manuscript.

Hour, Date, Place	Summary of Events and Information	Remarks and references to Appendices
6.45 a.m.	Slowed down to Battery fire 2 minute	
1.55 p.m.	Slowed down to 20 rds per hour	
3.45 p.m.	Under orders from Corps enemy works behind HOHENZOLLERN REDOUBT kept under constant fire at rate of 30 rds H.E per hour to prevent work being done on them.	R.O.C.
5th October	[crossed out] 83rd Infantry Brigade relieved 83rd Infantry Brigade.	R.O.C.
12.10 p.m.	Fire maintained all day as ordered. Fire reduced to 15 rounds per hour.	
6th October	2nd Guards Brigade relieved 83rd Infantry Brigade.	R.O.C.
	[crossed out] Fire maintained as above	
7th October	F.O.O. sent forward & line laid to H.Q. 3rd Grenadier Guards. Fire maintained as above	R.O.C.

Army Form C. 2118.

WAR DIARY
or
INTELLIGENCE SUMMARY.
(Erase heading not required.)

Instructions regarding War Diaries and Intelligence Summaries are contained in F.S. Regs., Part II. and the Staff Manual respectively. Title pages will be prepared in manuscript.

Hour, Date, Place	Summary of Events and Information	Remarks and references to Appendices
8th October 12 noon.	Enemy opened a heavy artillery fire on communication & support trenches on our front. Our rate of fire at once increased in retaliation.	
3.30 pm	Reopened bombardment all afternoon. Enemy attacked BIG WILLIE and got into a portion of it but were immediately driven back.	RDC
9 pm.	Fire reduced to normal rate of 15 rounds an hour.	
9th October	G.O.C. 2nd Guards Brigade reports that 18th & 62nd Batteries did great execution among the enemy returning to the attack. Normal rate of fire maintained day and night.	ROC
10th October 7 pm.	Normal rate of fire. A rapid burst of fire from 18th, 22nd, 62nd Batteries as the enemy were reported advancing to the attack.	

(73989) W4141—463. 400,000. 9/14. H.&J.Ltd. Forms/C. 2118/10.

Army Form C. 2118.

WAR DIARY
or
INTELLIGENCE SUMMARY.
(Erase heading not required.)

Instructions regarding War Diaries and Intelligence Summaries are contained in F. S. Regs., Part II. and the Staff Manual respectively. Title pages will be prepared in manuscript.

Hour, Date, Place	Summary of Events and Information	Remarks and references to Appendices
7.20 p.m.	Normal rate of fire resumed as the above proved a false alarm	
8.25 p.m.	18th Battery fired battery fire at a rapid rate gradually slowing down, to support a bombing attack by own infantry. The fire was to form a barrage	
11.30 p.m.	18th Battery resumed normal rate as original target as the attack was reported entirely successful and had captured the length of trench required.	R.O.C.
11th October	Normal fire, all day	
12th October 5 p.m.	Normal fire. Fire at an increased rate, as an enemy attack was reported. This proved a false alarm and it	R.O.C.
7 p.m.	Normal fire was resumed	

(73989) W4141—463. 400,000. 9/14. H.&J.Ltd. Forms/C. 2118/10.

WAR DIARY
or
INTELLIGENCE SUMMARY.
(Erase heading not required.)

Army Form C. 2118.

Instructions regarding War Diaries and Intelligence Summaries are contained in F.S. Regs., Part II. and the Staff Manual respectively. Title pages will be prepared in manuscript.

Hour, Date, Place	Summary of Events and Information	Remarks and references to Appendices
13th October		
12 noon	Bombardment commenced to prepare for an attack by 46th Division. A forward observing officer, accompanied the O.C. Right Counter battery, left brigade (went to GILES 18 at Battery.	
2 p.m.	Fire lifted to 2nd Phase. The first portion of the infantry advance appeared successful, but as they were held up beyond this.	
3 p.m.	The 2nd Phase was extended till 3pm. The fire was lifted to 3rd Phase, on a report from the infantry that they were consolidating their final objective. This was not borne out by artillery observers who reported	R.G.

WAR DIARY
or
INTELLIGENCE SUMMARY.

Army Form C. 2118.

Hour, Date, Place	Summary of Events and Information	Remarks and references to Appendices
8pm	our infantry held up in several places. Fire was continued till 8pm on Third Phase, and then as it was reported that our enemy only held the REDOUBT HOHENZOLLERN fire was taken the REDOUBT HOHENZOLLERN fire was brought back on to the Communication trenches leading into this REDOUBT from the enemy's position. Fire was maintained all night at 20 rounds per hour. One telephonist Driver of 18" Battery with F.O.O. wounded. Note as above	
(2)	Communication was maintained without a hitch all day from OPs to batteries & from Brigade H.Q. to Batteries. The reports of observing officers appear to have been most accurate, and this was the only accurate information received by the D division "knowtse" but were not correct but only reports were very optimistic but were not correct	

Army Form C. 2118.

WAR DIARY
or
INTELLIGENCE SUMMARY.
(Erase heading not required.)

Instructions regarding War Diaries and Intelligence Summaries are contained in F. S. Regs., Part II. and the Staff Manual respectively. Title pages will be prepared in manuscript.

Hour, Date, Place	Summary of Events and Information	Remarks and references to Appendices
	Communication with the F.O.O was not maintained, and it was impossible for runners to work along the communication trenches as they were packed with our troops. The brigade lines were very carefully pegged in low down along the communication trenches, but in spite of this they were torn down continually.	
(C)	A good deal of trouble was caused in batteries with the runny type fuse. Every opportunity of a slow rate of fire was seized to put guns out of action one at a time & overhaul them, but this throws a great strain on the remaining guns.	
	Ammunition expended by brigade was 2906 shrapnel and 2293 H.E.	

Army Form C. 2118.

WAR DIARY
or
INTELLIGENCE SUMMARY.
(Erase heading not required.)

Instructions regarding War Diaries and Intelligence Summaries are contained in F.S. Regs., Part II. and the Staff Manual respectively. Title pages will be prepared in manuscript.

Hour, Date, Place	Summary of Events and Information	Remarks and references to Appendices
14th October		
5.15 a.m.	Increased rate of fire to support our infantry attacking a trench junction.	
11.45 a.m.	This was maintained with variations in rate. Normal rate of fire 15 rds an hour continued.	
2.25 p.m.	365 Battery opened fire on a German working party who were showing themselves well above the trenches and stopped their activities.	R.P.i.
5.45 p.m.	Normal rate increased to 20 rds an hour.	
6.45 p.m.	18th Battery commenced rapid fire on communication trench to assist a bombing attack.	
8 p.m.	18th resumed normal rate. Normal rate was kept up all night. Ammunition expended 246 of shrapnel 15.61 HE.	
15 October		
2.25pm & 6.45pm	365 fired on LITTLE WILLIE every normal rate?	R.P.a.
	Enemy WILLIE to stop bomber who were standing up in the trench.	

(73989) W4141—463. 400,000. 9/14. H.&J.Ld. Forms/C. 2118/10.

Army Form C. 2118.

WAR DIARY
or
INTELLIGENCE SUMMARY.
(Erase heading not required.)

Instructions regarding War Diaries and Intelligence Summaries are contained in F.S. Regs., Part II. and the Staff Manual respectively. Title pages will be prepared in manuscript.

Hour, Date, Place	Summary of Events and Information	Remarks and references to Appendices
15th October	Normal rate of fire.	R.G.a.
2.15pm	18th & 22nd Batteries increased rate in retaliation for shelling of our trench.	
3.10pm	18th & 22nd reduced to normal rate.	
8.40pm	18th Battery increased rate to assist assault bombardment on 1 ot 60m of the HOHENZOLLERN REDOUBT	
11.30pm	18th Battery normal rate.	
17th October. 5am	All batteries opened fire at section five 30 rounds to cover bomb attack by 2nd & 3rd Grenade Brigades.	
6.50am	Enemy put heavy trench mortar & machine gun fire on our bombers on the slope. 62nd Battery was turned on to the SW corner at 2.30am.	

Army Form C. 2118.

WAR DIARY
or
INTELLIGENCE SUMMARY.
(Erase heading not required.)

Instructions regarding War Diaries and Intelligence Summaries are contained in F.S. Regs., Part II. and the Staff Manual respectively. Title pages will be prepared in manuscript.

Hour, Date, Place	Summary of Events and Information	Remarks and references to Appendices
10.30 a.m.	18th & 365th Batteries opened on DUMP TRENCH at Section fire 15 seconds to stop an expected counter attack.	RDC
2 p.m.	All batteries reduced to 20 rounds an hour.	RDC
	During the day 18th Battery had one gun with the muzzle blown off by premature H.E, but no casualties occurred, 62nd Battery had one gun out of action with a protruding A tube. Trouble was caused temporarily with damaged Inner Spring Cases, and Springs. Ammunition expended 2846 shrapnel, 2403 H.E.	
18th Oct.	All batteries fired on their normal fronts at normal rate till 3.15 p.m. when all Rodair Shooting was stopped	
3.15 p.m.		

WAR DIARY
or
INTELLIGENCE SUMMARY.
(Erase heading not required.)

Army Form C. 2118.

Hour, Date, Place	Summary of Events and Information	Remarks and references to Appendices
19th 9.15pm	Retaliation by 32nd 62nd & 366th on FOSSE COTTAGES - DUMP TRENCH was carried out. All firing was stopped at 6.15pm	
10.45pm	The enemy were discovered digging a new trench from Gd. 23. 9 n to Gd. 7. 6 n to Gd. 7. 10. 2. At 10.45pm all batteries opened fire on this trench with 2 rounds gun fire. The first round M.G.s short and each succession round at an increased range of 50 yds	ack
19th	No firing till 2.0pm when Batteries opened on normal line w/ 10 rounds per how	
5.15pm	Section Fire 15sec opened at 5.15pm on SOUTH FACE NORTH FACE DUMP TRENCH and NEW TRENCH to stop an attack on WEST FACE	
5.30pm	Normal Rate resumed	
5.45pm	Section Fire 15sec for 10 minutes, on POINT 97 - DUMP TRENCH ordered by CRA	
6.6pm	All Batteries resumed their normal low rate	ack

WAR DIARY
or
INTELLIGENCE SUMMARY.
(Erase heading not required.)

Army Form C. 2118.

Instructions regarding War Diaries and Intelligence Summaries are contained in F.S. Regs., Part II. and the Staff Manual respectively. Title pages will be prepared in manuscript.

Hour, Date, Place	Summary of Events and Information	Remarks and references to Appendices
19th	One section of 2nd battery came out of action having been relieved by Canadian Artillery	amR
20th	The A.C. and first section of 2nd battery marched to Concentration area at BUSNETTES amounting at illets found by billeting party at about 2.0 pm. Remaining sections arrived during the afternoon, the last to arrive at BUSNETTES being 1 23"Bty which arrived just after midnight after in advance of their new Gun Coverage at MERVILLE 15th Brigade out broke of man gr the 22nd Battery owing to the out break of man gr the 22nd Battery Suith 106 Battery	amR
21st	exchanged at Horace Farmiers & with 106 Battery 7th Division. 22nd, 63rd & 365th had exchanged their tired gun teams 146 Brigade who gave entraining cars day and therefore could not have spare overhauled. All guns overhauled by I.O.M. Great difficulty in getting Spares	amR

Army Form C. 2118.

WAR DIARY
or
INTELLIGENCE SUMMARY.
(Erase heading not required.)

Instructions regarding War Diaries and Intelligence Summaries are contained in F. S. Regs., Part II. and the Staff Manual respectively. Title pages will be prepared in manuscript.

Hour, Date, Place	Summary of Events and Information	Remarks and references to Appendices
22nd	The Brigade entrained at Killeen. The first train with 15th + half 22nd started at about 6 p.m. The 3rd Bank bgy 22 + 65 + at 4 o'c. 3rd with 26th + HQ at 7.6 p.m.	OMR
23rd	HQ entrained at Killeen	OMR
24th	On the train en route for Marseilles	OMR
25th	Arrived during night at Marseilles & marched to Camp at Pas Bouche. The last lot (HQ + 26) arriving camp at about 4.30 p.m. 26th October	OMR
26	In camp	OMR
27th	HQ Col arrived in camp about 7.30 a.m.	OMR
28th–31st	At Marseilles, nothing of interest. Preparing made up as for an overseas all Batteries made up to full strength in horses.	OMR

OMR Rodcliff RFA
OC 3rd Bde RFA

www.ingramcontent.com/pod-product-compliance
Lightning Source LLC
Chambersburg PA
CBHW081448160426
43193CB00013B/2411